Rock Music

Equipping a Band

By A. R. Schaefer

Consultant: James Henke
Vice President of Exhibitions and Curatorial Affairs
Rock and Roll Hall of Fame and Museum
Cleveland, Ohio

Capstone
press

Mankato, Minnesota

Capstone High-Interest Books are published by Capstone Press
151 Good Counsel Drive, P.O. Box 669, Mankato, Minnesota 56002
http://www.capstone-press.com

Copyright © 2004 by Capstone Press. All rights reserved.
No part of this publication may be reproduced in whole or in part, or stored in a retrieval
system, or transmitted in any form or by any means, electronic, mechanical,
photocopying, recording, or otherwise, without written permission of the publisher.
For information regarding permission, write to Capstone Press,
151 Good Counsel Drive, P.O. Box 669, Dept. R, Mankato, Minnesota 56002.
Printed in the United States of America

Library of Congress Cataloging-in-Publication Data
Schaefer, A. R. (Adam Richard), 1976–
    Equipping a band / by A. R. Schaefer.
    p. cm.—(Rock music library)
    Summary: Describes the steps involved in equipping a band, including choosing
instruments, making purchasing decisions, and the roles of the band's support staff.
    Includes bibliographical references (p. 31) and index.
    ISBN 0-7368-2145-7 (hardcover)
    1. Music trade—Vocational guidance—Juvenile literature. 2. Rock music—Vocational
guidance—Juvenile literature. [1. Bands (Music) 2. Rock music—Vocational guidance.
3. Music trade—Vocational guidance. 4. Vocational guidance.] I. Title. II. Series.
ML3790.S279 2004
784.4'166—dc21   2002155924

Editorial Credits
Carrie Braulick, editor; Jason Knudson; series designer; Jo Miller, photo researcher;
    Karen Risch, product planning editor

Photo Credits
Capstone Press/Gary Sundermeyer, cover, 5, 9, 11, 12, 13, 14, 15, 17, 18, 19, 20, 22,
    23 (all), 25, 28, 29
Corbis, 6; Matthew Mendelsohn, 21; Jacques M. Chenet, 27

Capstone Press thanks Rhapsody Music for their help in preparing this book.

1 2 3 4 5 6 08 07 06 05 04 03

Table of Contents

CHAPTER 1

What a Rock Band Needs

The stage is dark and empty. One by one, people carry and roll large black boxes to the middle of the stage. They open the boxes to show drums, guitars, speakers, amplifiers, and lights. The road and technical crews work to get everything into place. The workers test all of the equipment. After the stage is set up, everyone leaves and the lights are shut off.

A few hours later, a rock band struts onto the stage. The crowd breaks into cheers. Spotlights hit the performers as they walk to their places. The drummer gets to his equipment first. He has a big bass drum, a snare drum, tom-toms, and many cymbals.

Learn about:

Setting up for a performance

Band equipment

Band support staff

Drum sets can include crash cymbals.

An electric guitar is one of the main instruments in rock bands.

Next, the bassist plugs his bass guitar into the amplifier. He taps his finger on the microphone to make sure it is on.

The lead guitar player takes his place on center stage. His guitar wails as he slides his fingers on the strings, and the crowd cheers again. The band begins playing its opening song.

Needs of a Band

A successful performance depends on good equipment. Instruments, amplifiers, microphones, and other electronics are all important to a rock band.

Besides good equipment, a band needs a group of people for support. Support people can help a band with business matters. Established bands may have managers, promoters, booking agents, lawyers, and personal assistants. Members of a beginning band often do many of these jobs themselves. Friends and people in the music industry can help beginning musicians make good decisions.

CHAPTER 2

Main Rock Instruments

A rock band's main instruments usually are an electric guitar, a bass guitar, and a drum set. Band members should carefully select equipment. Some band members talk to music store owners, friends, and other people for advice on choosing instruments.

Many band members buy new instruments, but people also can find high-quality used instruments. Band members can find ads for used instruments in newspapers, on music store or school bulletin boards, or on the Internet.

Learn about:

Rock instruments

Equipment features

Price ranges

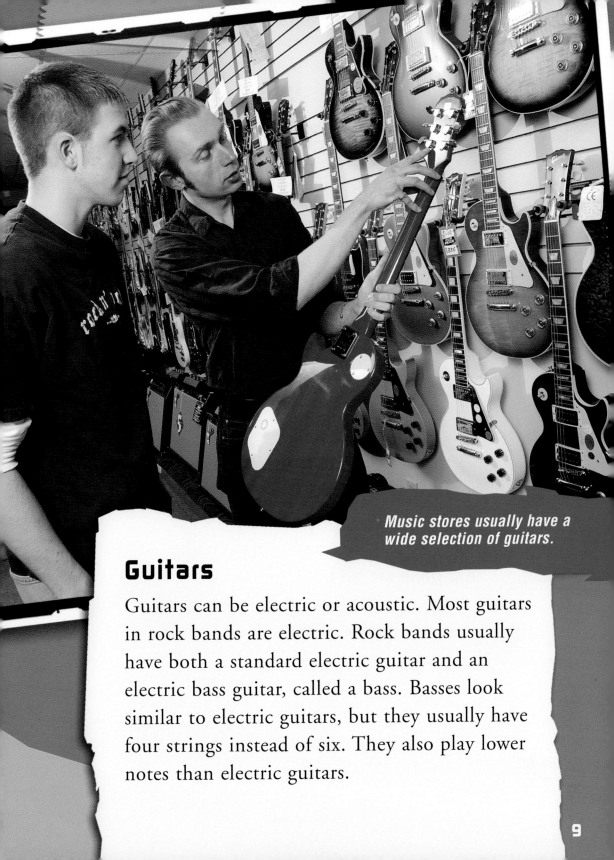

Music stores usually have a wide selection of guitars.

Guitars

Guitars can be electric or acoustic. Most guitars in rock bands are electric. Rock bands usually have both a standard electric guitar and an electric bass guitar, called a bass. Basses look similar to electric guitars, but they usually have four strings instead of six. They also play lower notes than electric guitars.

Several companies make electric guitars and basses. Common brand names include Fender, Gibson, Yamaha, Jackson, Ibanez, and Washburn. Electric guitars and bass guitars usually cost between $250 and $800. Some can cost thousands of dollars.

Some guitar companies make "starter sets" for beginning guitar players. These sets usually include a guitar, an amplifier, a guitar strap, and a tuner. Starter sets may be available for less than $300.

Guitar players should try out a guitar before they buy it. Each guitar has a unique sound. Some music stores have separate rooms available for people to try out instruments. Guitarists should make sure there are no buzzing noises coming from the guitar strings. They should like the sound of the guitar and feel comfortable holding it.

Guitarists should try out a guitar before buying it.

"One of my limitations is that it's hard for me to talk about guitar playing. I just do what I am capable of, which is not much."

—Billie Joe Armstrong, lead singer and guitarist of Green Day

Drum Sets

A rock band's drum set, or drum kit, has several drums and cymbals. A drum kit usually includes a bass drum, tom-tom drums, a snare drum, a pair of cymbals, and a hi-hat cymbal. Some sets include more drums and specialty instruments, such as wood blocks. Drum kits usually cost between $800 and $5,000, but starter sets may cost as little as $400. Common brand names are Ludwig, Gretsch, Yamaha, Pearl, and Tama.

Drummers should look over a drum set carefully before buying it.

Cymbals come in a variety of sizes.

Drummers should try out a drum set before buying it. They should make sure the set has well-balanced sound. No drum should be much louder than another. Drummers also should consider the set's type of wood. The least expensive sets usually are made of plywood. The most expensive sets usually are made of birch or maple wood. These types of wood produce a better sound.

More Instrument Choices

Some bands have instruments other than a drum set and guitars. A popular band called Blues Traveler is well known for the lead singer's harmonica skills.

Some rock bands include electronic keyboards. Keyboards have a variety of features. They have sounds programmed into them. Keyboards vary in price depending on their features. They can cost $500 to thousands of dollars. Yamaha and Casio are two well-known electronic keyboard manufacturers.

Many electronic keyboards have about 60 keys.

Musicians' hands should rest comfortably on a keyboard.

CHAPTER 3

Other Equipment

A band needs equipment in addition to its instruments. Guitar players need amplifiers. Singers need a microphone and a PA system. Many musicians have accessories for their instruments.

Guitar Amplifiers

Both electric guitars and basses need an amplifier. Amps make guitars sound louder and change the sound. Guitarists should bring their guitar along when buying an amp. They can plug their guitar into the amp to see if they like the sound.

Guitarists can choose solid-state, tube, or digital amplifiers. Solid-state amplifiers are useful for instruments that need to be

Learn about:

Amps

Microphones

Accessories

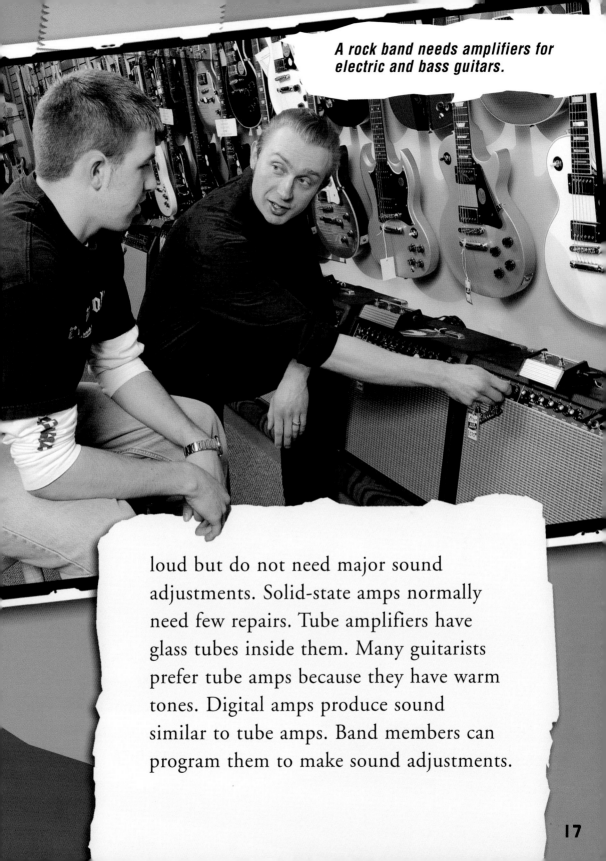

A rock band needs amplifiers for electric and bass guitars.

loud but do not need major sound adjustments. Solid-state amps normally need few repairs. Tube amplifiers have glass tubes inside them. Many guitarists prefer tube amps because they have warm tones. Digital amps produce sound similar to tube amps. Band members can program them to make sound adjustments.

The power of an amp is measured in watts. Amps with low wattage are quieter than amps with high wattage. An amp with 30 to 50 watts is usually enough for beginning guitar players. Some guitarists prefer to use amps with 100 watts or more.

Common amplifier brand names include Fender, Marshall, Crate, and Ampeg. Amps usually cost between $200 and $800. Beginners can get a basic model for about $400.

Musicians can buy solid-state amps (left) or tube amps (right).

Microphones

Bands need microphones. Both singers and instruments can have microphones. Band members sometimes plug microphones into amps.

Band members can buy dynamic or capacitor microphones. Dynamic microphones are durable and easily pick up loud sounds. Capacitor microphones are also called condenser microphones. Capacitor microphones are more sensitive than dynamic microphones. They pick up quiet sounds and high notes.

Band members usually choose dynamic models. Popular dynamic microphones are the Shure SM57 and SM58. Singers often use the SM58. Band members often use the SM57 with an instrument. Both models cost about $100.

The SM58 (left) and SM57 (right) are two popular microphones.

Band members consider price, wattage, and other features when buying a PA system.

PA Systems

Most bands need a PA system so singers can be heard. PA systems usually include a microphone, or PA head, and two speakers. Band members plug the singers' microphones into the PA system. Some bands also plug instruments into a PA system.

Fender, Yamaha, Peavey, and Samson are some PA system manufacturers. PA systems can range in price from $500 to $3,000.

The Dave Matthews Band

The Dave Matthews Band has been one of the most popular bands of the late 1990s and early 2000s. The band is named after the lead singer, Dave Matthews. Matthews is also a guitarist and songwriter.

The Dave Matthews Band formed in Charlottesville, Virginia. In 1991, Matthews decided to record some of his songs on a tape. He hired musicians to help him record his songs. The band included an electric guitar player, bassist, drummer, saxophone player, keyboardist, and violinist. The band's first gig was for a private party. Later that year, the group played at a local festival. The band soon gained fans.

In 1993, the band made its first album. The album went gold. It sold more than 500,000 copies. Later albums sold even more copies. The group's concerts have been sold out around the world.

Instrument Accessories

Band members buy accessories for their instruments. Guitarists have spare guitar picks, strings, and straps. Drummers have a variety of drumsticks.

Some guitarists use equipment to create different musical effects. They may use fuzz tone pedals. Guitar players can step on a fuzz tone pedal while playing. The pedal increases the guitar's volume and makes its tone sound less clear, or fuzzy. A wah pedal is similar to a fuzz tone pedal. It changes the tone of a guitar when the guitarist steps on it.

Drummers need drumheads for their set. These plastic coverings fit over one or both ends of a drum. Drumheads come in different thicknesses. Some drumheads are designed to produce a unique type of sound.

Fuzz tone and wah pedals change the tone of a guitar.

Band members need accessories, such as guitar straps, strings, picks, and drumsticks.

CHAPTER 4

Band Support

In addition to good equipment, a band needs the support of many people to be successful. Music store workers, sound and light technicians, managers, and friends can all be sources of help.

Beginning bands often have friends and family members help them with support activities. Friends may help a band set up or pass out promotional fliers at a gig. Sometimes friends and family members come to many of a band's gigs. They can help create excitement in the audience as the band performs.

Learn about:

Managers

Business professionals

Technical professionals

Music store workers can support band members by helping them choose equipment.

Handling Business Duties

Beginning bands usually handle many business duties on their own. One band member may act as the group's manager. A manager is in charge of all of a band's business duties. The manager books gigs, manages money, and handles promotion.

Other duties may include setting up interviews with radio and TV stations, producing fliers, and selling T-shirts at gigs.

Established bands often hire several people to perform business duties. Booking agents help bands receive new gigs. Promoters organize and run live shows. Publicists create a good public image for bands. They make press releases, press kits, and other materials that can be passed out to media members. Business managers handle a band's money. Music lawyers help bands make legal agreements.

Technical Professionals

Some bands hire people to help them develop their sound or make their performances more exciting. Sound technicians adjust audio settings at gigs. Light technicians develop lighting arrangements for shows.

Well-established bands travel to gigs in different locations. These bands sometimes have a road crew and a technical crew. The road crew helps move the band's equipment from gig to gig. The technical crew sets up the sound system and lights for each show.

Sound technicians are trained to run soundboards and other sound equipment.

Band members carefully select people to support them. They want their support staff to help them become better musicians, perform better shows, and become more popular. Obtaining a good support staff is an important step for bands that want to make it big.

Caring for a Guitar

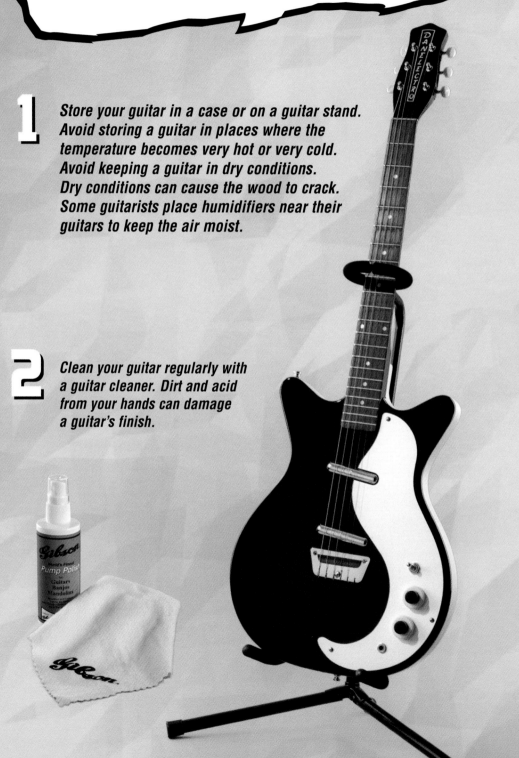

1 Store your guitar in a case or on a guitar stand. Avoid storing a guitar in places where the temperature becomes very hot or very cold. Avoid keeping a guitar in dry conditions. Dry conditions can cause the wood to crack. Some guitarists place humidifiers near their guitars to keep the air moist.

2 Clean your guitar regularly with a guitar cleaner. Dirt and acid from your hands can damage a guitar's finish.

3 *Wipe down your guitar with a soft cloth each time you finish using it.*

4 *Replace worn or dirty strings.*

Glossary

acoustics (uh-KOO-stiks)—dealing with the way a room reflects sound; rooms with good acoustics allow people to hear music clearly.

amplifier (AM-pluh-fye-ur)—a piece of equipment that makes sound louder; an amplifier also can change sound.

booking agent (BUK-ing AY-juhnt)—someone who sets up gigs for a band

drumhead (DRUM-hed)—the material stretched over one or both ends of a drum

flier (FLY-ur)—a printed piece of paper that tells about an upcoming gig

gig (GIG)—a job for a musician or a band to play in public

promoter (pruh-MOTE-ur)—someone who organizes live shows for a band

publicist (PUB-luh-sist)—someone who works to develop a positive public image for a band

watt (WOT)—a unit for measuring electrical power

To Learn More

Anjou, Erik. *Dave Matthews Band.* Galaxy of Superstars. Philadelphia.: Chelsea House, 2002.

Erlewine, Dan. *How to Make Your Electric Guitar Play Great!: The Electric Guitar Owner's Manual.* A Guitar Player Book. San Francisco: Backbeat Books, 2001.

Morgan, Sally, and Pauline Lalor. *Music.* Behind Media. Chicago: Heinemann Library, 2001.

Useful Addresses

Rock and Roll Hall of Fame and Museum
One Key Plaza
Cleveland, OH 44114

RockWalk
7425 Sunset Boulevard
Hollywood, CA 90046

Rolling Stone Magazine
1290 Avenue of the Americas
New York, NY 10104-0298

Internet Sites

Do you want to find out more about rock bands?
Let FactHound, our fact-finding hound dog, do the research for you.

Here's how:

1) Visit *http://www.facthound.com*
2) Type in the **Book ID** number: **0736821457**
3) Click on **FETCH IT**.

**FactHound will fetch Internet sites picked by our editors
just for you!**

Index